THE GOOD MISTRESS

THE BEST KEPT SECRET

KHALILAH SMITH
and
DANI ALEXANDER

This book reflects the views of the author. We are in no way suggesting or defending a certain lifestyle. This book is based on opinions and also includes excerpts of fiction. Any similarities to actual people or places are purely coincidental.

Copyright© 2015 by Dream Out Loud Productions with KK's World. All rights reserved. No part of this book may be reproduced in any form except for the inclusion of a brief quotation in a review without permission in writing from the authors or publisher.
Cover Design by Free Creatives

Follow The Good Mistress:
Twitter: good_mistress
Instagram: good_mistress

Printed in the United States

First Edition: May 2015

THE GOOD MISTRESS

Air

THE GOOD MISTRESS

Prelude: Message from a Mistress

Introduction: History of Mistresses

Chapter 1: The Good, The Bad, The Difference 1

Chapter 2: Loyalty... 15

Chapter 3: Signs.. 21

Chapter 4: The Look.. 31

Chapter 5: Rules of Engagement....................... 41

Chapter 6: Her Role... 57

Chapter 7: What He Said................................... 71

Chapter 8: From Guilty to Forgiven................... 79

Chapter 9: A Good Mistress' Apology................ 97

Chapter 10: Dear, Good Mistress....................... 101

Chapter 11: Meditations.................................... 106

Chapter 12: Extras... 110

Message from a Mistress

Dear Mrs.,

I am your worst nightmare a.k.a. his mistress

I know everything about him, including you
While you sit in the dark without a clue

I know you feel my presence, ghostlike premonition
The emptiness in your gut is called woman's intuition

Allow me to introduce myself; I am Bae, his Mami,
His sweetheart too
I get the same, I miss you, I need you, I love you boo

But trust, I don't want to be you

Understudy I am not.
While you're nervous questioning, I am comfy
In my spot

You can act like you don't know, but in your head there's a little voice

My security is in knowing, and in knowing I have a choice
And I chose him, well he chose me
I had idea he was your man or was supposed to be.

This is not an attempt to hurt you. You're not a factor in my equation.

I am not a bad person, just in a bad situation.
I won't insult you with sorry, but I do apologize.
I love that man, and I did before I even realized, that
Secret lovers would be our pact,
More like his best "kept" secret in fact

Before you wake he jogs, you take that to be his way
But his call log will show my good morning is his 1st
Of every day

I share all his smiles of joy, his cried tears of frustrations
His dreaded business trips for you, were some of my best vacations.

You got him on lock through loyalty, but through love
Me he yearns.
I'm all in, prepared for when karma returns.

And with that thought in mind, I've tried numerous times to leave
But your asthmatic antics, keeps him running back for my air to breathe

Dear Mrs.
This message is heartfelt but you will never get this
The truth in this scribe, he will never forgive this
So my lips are sealed with his kisses
I'll never tell; I am his good mistress.

INTRODUCTION

Mistresses have been around since the beginning of time. Since there have been marriages, there have been extramarital affairs. In every time period, every culture and every religion, there have been mistresses or its equivalent by different names, for example, Geishas, concubine, pilegesh.

A concubine is generally a woman in an ongoing matrimonial relationship with a man she cannot marry for a specific reason. That reason is usually because he is married already. In history and present day the relationship between a man and his mistress is one of stability and in most times there is an implication of the woman being "kept." This is what outsiders might perceive as hush money but that is not always the case. Just as she is his best kept secret, it is his pleasure to make sure that she is alright, financially and otherwise. Historically only men of high economic and social status had mistress. Certain Jewish thinkers believed that concubines were reserved for kings. Maybe this is why today, society has the misconception that all athletes, entertainers and men of upper echelon have mistress. THIS IS NOT TRUE, ALL RICH MEN DON'T HAVE A MISTRESS and

AFFAIRS CAN OCCUR IN EVERY TAX BRACKET! There is however a certain sense of arrogance that is required for a man to successfully carry on a relationship with a wife and a mistress. For many men, confidence is attached to their bank account and so the assumption is understood.

  Media and the misuse of the word "mistress" has created a terrible taboo for her existence. The mistress is always the one to blame. You see it on television and in real life, the woman in the affair is considered the bad person, and not the husband. She is considered "less than" the wife. However in biblical times the concubine commanded the same respect as the wife. In fact the wife had to pay dowry to her husband and the mistress did not. In Renaissance times, the Italian usage of the word "cortigiana" referred to the "ruler's mistress" that word was also used to describe a well-educated and independent woman of free morals, one associated with wealthy, powerful, or upper-class men who provided luxuries and status in exchange for companionship. Historically the mistress was never considered "less than!" This is not an attempt at GLORIFYING the life of a mistress rather an attempt to put it into perspective. Most of the women or men involved in this lifestyle did not wake up and choose this life. Most times the "Good Mistress" was fooled or betrayed too. So how do you blame a person for falling in love?

  This book is an attempt at exposing the other side of the spectrum. Forget what you see on television and what you've read about in all the high profile affair scandals. The **mistress** is not always the **bad person**, and **every woman that sleeps with a married man is not a mistress** (there are a number of names reserved for these women). Since extramarital affairs will always exist, we decided to view it through the eyes of the "Bad Guy", she is The Good Mistress…

THE GOOD, THE BAD,
THE DIFFERENCE

Since the "Tiger Woods" scandal, the word "mistress" has been grossly overused as well as misused. We were offended for him and the woman that might actually be Tiger's mistress for all the women that the media were labeling mistress. There definitely are levels to cheating. This section is a guide to breakdown the different women and relationships a man might have at different or concurrent times in his life. There is a hierarchy. The key thing is to know your role.

We took the liberty to list the titles and definitions in order from least importance to greatest (in most cases).

Prostitute/ Hooker: a person who provides sexual services to another person in return for payment. Known as the oldest profession in the world, hookers have far moved from just being women on corners or ladies of the night. This is big business camouflaged by the guise of VIP services and concierges. Prostitution is quite a lucrative business mainly because many men are looking for a no strings attached way to carryout extramarital sexual encounters.

Groupie: the groupie is a classic opportunist. She knows all the events that the men of the chosen field she is interested in will be. She knows all the club promoters and can get behind most velvet ropes. She is interested in the lime light. It doesn't matter who he is, as long as he is "somebody." Sex is definitely an option for her but she loves the light and wants most to say that she was with said person. Expert Groupies do their research. If the interest is athletes they know stats, schedules, injuries. If it's a politician they are interested in, they know policies, they attend rallies etc. For the church groupies, they volunteer for extra ministries, attend all workshops and most likely can quote every scripture in the Bible. Yes, pastors have groupies!

Jump-off: the jump-off may at one point have been or still is a groupie but not necessarily. She is a female that whenever business brings him to her city, she will probably get a call. The visit may consist of a date, sex, and all of the things that makes a woman feel like she is in a relationship. This relationship does carry some consistency however it consist of the visit. You may get to visit him on a road game or business trip in another city as well. He doesn't socially communicate with her unless he is in her town or planning a visit. He may have a jump-off in other cities as well.

Girlfriend: She is the woman that he is in an exclusive relationship with. They don't live together per say but there is a commitment. She may be dependent on him, he may pay all of her bills but they are "her" bills. They still maintain separate financial affairs. They "go together."

Wifey: Is the live in girlfriend or "main chick." She may be the fiancée. This is an exclusive relationship. They may share some credit, or bank accounts. Both of their names may be on the lease. She is close to being a wife but not quite yet.

Wife: Is a female partner in marriage. This is the woman with whom he took vows. She is thought to be a man's life partner. This is the ultimate exclusive relationship.

*Technically a man must have a wife in order for the mistress to exist, period point blank! This is debatable by most wifeys and girlfriends.

Baby Mama: She is just that, the mother of his child. This may be a good or bad relationship. She may be the ex wife or girlfriend. She may be a slip up with a groupie. However the baby came to be, the child's mother exists. She fits differently in the hierarchy; in dealing with a good man her role is important because she is raising his child.

The role of mistress was left off of this hierarchy chart. This is because like most hierarchy structures, the persons at the bottom are usually fighting for the role at the top. One of the biggest misconceptions is that the mistress wants to be his wife. The "Good Mistress" does not want to be his wife. She is comfortable in her role. Over time she has been the sounding board and the breath of fresh air that he runs to escape the perils of marriage, so why would she want that position. She is clear on what the relationship is. While the wife is at home wondering, the mistress knows. That is the Difference!

Not So Ordinary Love Story

When Sara fell in love with her Jr. High classmate, she knew it was for a lifetime. Sure, all teenagers say that, but Sara knew, and luckily Michael felt the same way. He was her first and only, she was his first, not last or only but that was just part of the growing pains of being with the same guy from the age of thirteen. It did not matter, because they weathered every storm. They did it right. They graduated, went to college, and during that time they married and shortly after began their family. They had three kids, two girls and a boy and Papi their dog. They both had careers, but Sara's real joy was having the flexibility to be home when her kids got off the school bus, to have dinner ready to greet her husband after work, after he greeted her with a kiss. Their life was perfect, down to the kid's games on Saturday, church on Sunday. She was busy loving her life that it never dawned on her that her life was all she knew. Loving Michael was the only love she knew and why would she long for anything else because it felt right.

It was an ordinary Wednesday, the kids were doing homework and the meatloaf had just come out the oven. Michael Jr. had a problem with his homework that was taking the assistance of Sara and his older sisters! Geesh, this new math is crazy! With the back and forth of the homework, she had not realized that Michael hadn't made it in from work. She did not worry at that point, but when she had to sit the kids down for dinner without their dad, and his phone calls were going to voicemail, Sara knew something was not right. Still the consummate mom, she did not show her kids that she was worried. When they asked "where is daddy," she told a white lie and stated he had late meetings. When she answered the phone displaying a private number, all she heard was "Mrs. Hunter, there's been an accident!"

Dinner was on the table at 5:30pm, at the normal time the week following the funeral. Carpool leader for Michaela's volleyball team resumed, Michael Jr,'s Basketball practices and games on time, Mia's piano lesson check, and homework and school activities done! All Sara knew, was how to be a mother and wife, and yes although her husband had passed away in a terrible accident, she was still a ring wearing wife! Two years passed of the same routine, dinner time altered from time to time due to a practice schedule, but life carried on. Yes, sleepless nights, and crying to daybreak occurred but by the time she would awake the smiling faces of her three angels, it always dissipated. It would be a June trip to Disneyworld with their grandparents that offered the first break from being a mom since she gave birth. The first night was all tears, and resisting getting on the plane to Florida to get her babies, but on the 2nd night, her cousin persuaded her to step out to a sports bar and watch the NBA Finals. She felt like a fish out of water, and although she was only 29, she was a widowed mother of 3, she did not belong. So it actually annoyed her when men approached her, especially since she still wore a wedding ring. However, she was enjoying the game, she was enjoying not ordering for the kids, and just thinking of what she wanted to eat or drink. She enjoyed it so much that it brought her to tears, tears that she quickly caught before anyone noticed and caused a scene. She did not realize how tired she had been and at the moment of relief she felt guilty. "Hey Brook, I'm gonna run to the bathroom." She wanted to freshen up, although no one had noticed her mini melt down.

"So you must be a Laker fan?" "Excuse me?" "I saw you drop a tear, don't trip it sucks having a weak team huh!" Laughter, she had not had pure adult laughter in such a long time. "I am not a Laker fan, and clearly you were looking at me too hard" she said with a smile. "I am John, I am actually a Laker fan" he extended his hand to shake, and Sara being a lefty, she extended her left hand to greet his handshake and he said "and you are married!" "I am Sara, and yes it is a very complicated situation, but thank you for noticing." Sara returned to her table with her cousin, and shortly after, the waitress brought over a round of drinks from John. After the game, when we waited to settle our tab, the waitress informed us that it had also been settled by John. She had a message from him; he said to let Sara know that he will pray that what is complex becomes clear. The cousins looked around to thank him, but he was gone.

It was amazing how just that evening out, some attention from the opposite sex made a difference in the burden of life that Sara was shouldering. Her kids returned from vacation and life carried on. On an evening a few weeks later, Sara's cousin was in the same sports bar as before and she was approached by a gentleman. "Hello; how's Sara?" Her cousin looked shocked. "You know my cousin?" She responded. The guy explained that he didn't really know her, but he met her a few weeks ago when they were there, he told her that he was John. Sara's cousin thanked him for his treat, and she explained that Sara doesn't get out much, and that her outing was a rarity and a first since her husband passed away a couple of years ago. This explained what was complex to him. John asked for her to tell Sara he said hello, and to give her his number just in case rarity strikes again.

It was an ordinary summer night, the kids had laid down for bed and Sara sat in her bed watching the 11 pm edition of Sports Center before she drifted off into dreamland. She read across the ticker breaking news of a signing of a big name player for the Lakers. "Shut up!" She said aloud to herself. Without thought she reached for the number that had been sitting on her nightstand and dialed it.

"Hello"

"Hi, is this John?"

"Yes"

"This is Sara, did you see who your team just got?!"

It was 2 am when Sara forced herself to end the best conversation she had in forever. It was 5 am for him, during the conversation Sara found out that John had been on the West Coast for business when they met but he actually lived in Atlanta. He was also a few years younger than she; he had one son, and was a graduate of the University of North Carolina. She had decided that John would be like a little brother, he was funny and cool but she was not looking for anything more, plus he was too young for her. At any rate, she went to sleep with a smile on her face.

To fast forward this story because this is just a small segment of this book, the two began to talk daily. Sara was old-school and was used to talking on the phone, but when she realized in order to protect her kids from the fact that mom was talking to a guy, she opted on texting mostly. His job had brought him back to the West Coast for the season, so they were also able to spend time hanging out. And then one night, while talking on the phone, he told her that she needs some sexual relief in her life. She responded with a joking "shut up!" Strangely she wasn't offended, but what that did was open a window for a different level of conversation. Conversation that was not brother and sisterly!

December brought the end of the season, and after a farewell dinner, their relationship changed. As they lay in each other arms, looking up at the ceiling, he asked the inevitable. "So what are we? I am in love with you Sara."

Sara sat quietly for a moment, she had fallen in love with him as well, but a relationship was not in her cards. "I love you too John, I enjoy our time, but right now I am not ready to put a title on what we are. Whatever we are, whatever this is, I want it. I am just not ready to call it anything."

When he returned to Atlanta, everything seemed the same. They still talked a couple of times a day, sometimes his son would be in the background, and they also texted when her kids were around. He seemed to have a good relationship with his son's mom, which she appreciated and respected. Whatever John and Sara had, it was growing. He visited her once a month and they met for a vacation get away in Hawaii. He was her breath of fresh air. He adored her. He was her ounce of selfishness; she did not have to be anything but Sara when she was with him. So imagine how she felt when she returned home and went on his Facebook to send him an inbox message (yes they were Facebook friends) and to read a post on his wall from a family member of his saying Congrats on the new baby.

"Is there something you need to tell me?" She calmly asked John when he called her that night. "I been trying to tell you, I wanted to tell you in Hawaii, I'm sorry." It all sounded like the teacher on Charlie Brown to Sara, as tears rolled down her face. She heard him say it was before they got together, that was probably true, she heard him say that he was in love with her; she believed that, she also heard him say it was a fluke when she picked up their son. "Oh, so the baby is by your son's mom, your college sweetheart?" She had heard enough, so she hung up the phone. She did not care that he had a baby on the way; the timeframe was aligned with it being before they hooked up. She was hurt that he had not told her. After days of unanswered calls, and being unhappy, she missed her joy. She missed her ounce of selfishness, so when he called on that day, she answered. She tried to return to platonic friendship mode, even encouraging him to salvage the relationship with his kid's mom. It was going to be work going back, but she enjoyed him being in her life. The next day he was on the plane to make sure they were good, and the next day, they were back to that thing, whatever it was.

    This relationship existed for a couple of years. She never visited him because she still was still number one, a mom and she did not like leaving her children. When she did on a rare occasion, he always convinced her that going to an exotic location would be a better get away than coming to Atlanta, and she agreed. During their relationship, he asked her on occasion about becoming more than a special friend; he asked her if she would marry again. She would always answer that her one marriage was for her lifetime, and she was happy to never marry again. She was content, she had companionship when need be, her kids were happy and their life was not disrupted, and she had her little bit of selfishness.

One random Friday evening Sara got a call from John. He didn't sound himself. He said he was back in North Carolina for a family function, but he did not sound excited. She asked if his babies were with him, he told her that they were there, and their mom (he said her name). They talked for a while, but Sara felt something in her stomach that something was not right with him. She asked,

"So what kind of family function is it, maybe I will fly down?"

"Oh how I wish it were you here with me."

"Well you know how family can be" she answered.

He replied, "exactly, it's all for family."

She found an excuse to get off the phone, nothing was said directly, but she knew what was happening without the words. When she got off the phone he texted her and said, just say the word and I won't. Sara told him that she could not save him from himself, and congratulations. It seemed like everything she loved, she lost. She thought about calling to stop him, but she knew she really didn't want to marry him. She wanted what they were, a few stolen moments to remain. She decided to delete him from the phone and her life. The next day she was uneasy, she wondered if it was a day wedding, or an evening wedding. Where would they go on the honeymoon, she had way too much idle time. When her phone rang from a 404 number she nervously answered.

"Hey Babe"

She sat on the phone frozen. Was he a run-away groom? Why was he calling her?

"You there?"

"Yes I am here, why are you calling me, shouldn't you be jumping the broom or something?'

"I'm sorry"

"Don't. What do you want?"

"I call you every night don't I? I have to remind you to take your iron pills. Have you?"

She hadn't.

"Thank you, I did. I don't need you to do that for me anymore." She began to cry silently. "Everything I love, I lose."

"Everything is not always what it seems, and I am here, I will always be here."

John and Sara's relationship was different. Sara was not a bad person; she did not seek out this man that was in a relationship. John was not a bad guy either. The story does not show how he came from a strict religious family that set certain pressures on him to do certain things, like marry his children's mom. It is so easy to say that Sara should have ended their relationship on that day when he called from his reception, but love is not easy. She was in love with this man, and she did not know his wife. She had experienced such loss, that he was her lifeline and she was not ready to drown again.

LOYALTY

Mistresses are **loyal**. One may believe it is a crazy idea. The very essence of her existence is based on deceit. However for the "Good Mistress," knowing that although her deeds may be considered vile and dark to many, it is the **loyalty** and love for her guy that is the only shining light in the darkness of this arrangement.

Loyalty is one of the key factors in a successful relationship. This factor is not absent in the success of the relationship of a mistress and her man. **Loyalty** is faithfulness, it is allegiance, it is an obligation to defend and support another, even when at times that person is wrong. **Loyalty** is the catch twenty-two of an extramarital affair. Sometimes, the love is lost in a marriage, but because of loyalty the husband (or wife) will remain in the relationship. However, that same **loyalty** does not stop them from falling in love with another individual. Then there is the mistress, perhaps unknowingly, she falls in love with this man, but once she does, and becomes loyal, she too is stuck. **Loyalty** will prevent the Good Mistress from ever doing anything that would cause her man unhappiness, even if it means maintaining a secret relationship.

"Will you take this woman to be your wedded wife? Will you love and comfort her, honor and keep her, in sickness and in health, forsaking all others, keep yourself only unto her, for as long as you both shall live?"

The above vows are pretty standard. Some of the words may differ from wedding to wedding but the main points remain the same. He made a vow to her! Mistresses are so often labeled the "home wrecker," when in fact another woman should not be able to wreck her home. Most times, the proverbial "home" that is being wrecked, was already on a shaky foundation. In an affair, the married person is the only bulldozer that can wreck the home.

Somehow, this unwritten rule was created that women are supposed to look out for every other woman in the world. Why? People do not come equipped with that sort of sensor on their heart. If a person falls in love with a man, even if it was under false pretenses, it is unrealistic for that love to automatically shut off if some ugly truth is brought to light. When time, energy and love have been invested in a man, and she doesn't know his wife, the loyalty ball is more apt to drop in that man's court and not his wife whom she has no relation with. Although it sounds good when it best suits our own personal needs as women; it actually is not a character flaw if we don't always "look out for a sister!"

Many relationships are suffering from what we will call the "Alicia Keys" syndrome. We must note that we do not know anything about Alicia Keys except that she is an amazing artist and what was played out in the media about how she got her man. WE DO NOT believe the media! However we use that term to make a point. This syndrome is when a marriage is over via functionality, but is hanging on technically. As much as we want to believe in the fairytale of happily ever after, sometimes people's feelings change. With no reason or rhyme, sometimes people just wake up one morning and feel different. We are all human, and change is a human right. Is it fair to make someone stay in a miserable situation when someone else makes them happy? Times have changed. Marriages are a business. You have money, property, kids and even a reputation of the "business" at stake. Walking away from the business of a marriage is not as easy as some may think. If you know that your husband is no longer in love with you, (trust, most times women know and it has been openly discussed), should he deny the happiness another woman brings him because at the time, the business affairs created while married are not in order yet? On the other side of this syndrome, regardless of what he does, and if it's right or wrong, why is this other woman (hypothetically Alicia Keys) obligated to put her happiness on hold while the wife attempts to salvage something that is already lost? We call this "AK" syndrome because a million women were mad at "AK" for becoming involved and later marrying a guy who was allegedly married when they started dating. The ex-wife did all she could to smear the name of "AK" stating that they were involved while they were still married etc. We do not know these people, but watching this play out on television it was clear that this man was no longer in love with ex-wife. At this point, does it matter who he is with? Your beef should not be about that. We understand being hurt that he is no longer in love with you, but who he falls in love with, after he fell out of love with you is irrelevant. What we do know is that "AK" has done a great deal of good for the world through her service and charity. Was she a mistress? Maybe. Is she a bad person? Highly unlikely!

There is a big difference between the bond of a marriage and that of a mistress and her man. A marriage is legal, there are papers that bind it, and so it operates as law because it is. The Good Mistress and her man operate according to a "code." A "code" is unwritten, but it is understood by all parties. If you break a law on your job, you may be punished, written up, or fired. But in the hood, in the locker room, on a team, in the military, in life, if you break the code, you are condemned! "Codes" are based on Loyalty!

SIGNS

As we have stated, the "GM" does not go into a relationship with a married man with intentions of hurting anyone. Most times, in the beginning the "GM" is unaware that her man is married. There are some women functioning as a mistress, reading this book and they don't know they are a mistress at all. Here's a little tip, if you are out with a group of single girlfriends (or married friends) look around, one out of the crew is someone's mistress and it just might be you. We have compiled a list of tips that may be a "tell tale" sign that you are a mistress.

Friends over Family: If you have only been around certain friends, and have never met his family although they live in the same city as you. If he often speaks of his family, and how you remind him of his sister but never offers to introduce you all. If he lies and says he doesn't have family.

Holidays: Do you all celebrate all of the major holidays, especially Valentine's Day early or late? Does he say that he is not big on holidays, but he still seems to always splurge on your gift, kind of overcompensating for not spending the day with you? Is he MIA on these days?

Gifts: Does he tell you that you don't have to buy him anything for his birthday or holidays. Or if you do purchase him something, you never notice him wear it? Chances are, that gift never survived the light of day because to wear it, would draw unwanted suspicion from his wife.

The phone: Did he say he prefers to text? Does he call you at standard times (ie. during the day or commute home if he works a 9-5)? Does he every now and then call you at a random time, but seem nervous or anxious, and has to rush off the phone? (He is calling from the house but at any moment, wife can walk in). Do you get the phone call, and you can tell he is in the car in motion, and then he arrives at a destination and will talk a few moments more, but gets off before he gets out of the car? Does he not answer when you call outside of the before mentioned "standard times?"

The House: Have you ever been to his house? (There is an exception because some men are fully vested and have a honeycomb hideout apartment). If you have, does the apartment look almost like a hotel, no pictures, memorabilia, no life? This is the honeycomb hideout. Or did he say that he doesn't have people over his house because his ex may bring the kid over at anytime? Like even at 3'oclock in the morning? Has he never stayed over at your home? If he stays over, does it look like he packed for an out of town trip when you live in the same city? Guess what, his wife thinks he is away on business.

The Currency: When he opens his wallet do you see that he has plenty of credit cards but every transaction while with you are made with cash? If there is a situation where a credit card is absolutely needed for travel, rental purposes etc, will he give you the money and have you use your card? Has he given you a substantial amount of money to hold for him, when you know he has a bank? He is establishing trust and trying to make you feel like you are "the one," If he is not involved in the underworld, why else would he have you hold his money?

Day Trip: You both live in the city but he always wants to take day trips for your dates to neighboring cities a few hours away. "We have to go to that one restaurant with the great ambiance." Or have you all driven miles to catch a movie at the same theater that you all have located in the strip center down the street?

The Ex: Does the ex-girlfriend have so much control over his life that it overrides your position? When you question "why he is not with her" is he uncomfortable with answering. Does he tell you that she, his ex is sick? Or she has been there for him through so much so he feels a certain type of loyalty to her? Perhaps his ex is actually his current.

No Footprint: Does he not have or use any form of Social media? Or did you find that he had one, but he never disclosed that information to you. If he does have Twitter, Facebook, LinkedIn, or Instagram does he have his security settings so tight that you can only see his name and profile picture.

There is no need to feel naïve if you read the previous information and feel that you have had blinders on; you are not alone in this. It is important to figure if you want to continue in this relationship, have the conversation either way and proceed. The way he reacts and the result of the conversation will let you know if he considers you a mistress or if he considers you one of the other titles we mentioned earlier. (*See the Chapter "The Difference"*) When we say you are not alone, we mean in the naïve state. There are many wives reading this book, sitting at home saying, "not my man!" Yes, your man may have one too. The below tips are "tell tale" signs that you may be sharing him.

Sex: Are you finding that he is not trying to jump on it every opportunity he gets. Do you find yourself having to initiate intercourse? And has he denied you of his husbandly duties because he is tired or had a bad day at work? Do you know that sex is the best way to get over a bad day at work?

The Phone: Does his phone remain with him at all times? Is the ringer no longer on ring, but on vibrate? Does he often laugh out loud from a text received and then randomly say "John is crazy" to throw you off? If you by strange chance get a hold of his phone, is it some numbers stored by initials? Is his text log absolutely empty except for text between you all? Are you guys on separate phone plans or does the bill go to his office or business manager?

Running Errands: Did your husband use to hate to run to the store, but now he jumps at any chance to make a run without you? He will go on the tampon run, pick up dry-cleaning, the tomatoes you forgot at the store, and take the kid to ballet practice, because these are opportunities to talk to her. Do every now and then the errands take longer than usual? This could be due to a heated conversation with her or a quick drive by if she lives in the same city.

Business Trips: Has the dreaded business trip, turned into your husband volunteering for work related conferences and trips? Did he use to ask you to accompany him, but now discourage you? How about, "I won't be in the room much, so call me on my cell phone?" Perhaps, he is on the other side of town playing house and not actually on a business trip.

Can't get right: Has it become that no matter what you do, it seems to not be right, not be enough, or just doesn't make him happy? Does he seem to be reaching, accusing you, and sparking unwarranted arguments? It is not what you aren't doing; it is what someone else is doing. People, who are in the wrong, try their best to find fault in the other party to justify their doings.

Time Out: Does he suggest at first sign of disagreement that you guys should separate or consider divorce? Does he need space or time alone to clear his head?

No Invite: He now makes excuses why he doesn't want go to his friend's group events, or suggest that the party will probably be boring and insist that you wouldn't want to go. He offers alternative plans in exchange to throw you off of the radar of why you guys are not going to the yearly Christmas party you have attended your whole relationship. This is perhaps because he has since started dating the best friend or coworker of the wife of his friend and to have you all in one place would not be acceptable.

The Late Shift: Has y'all bedtime become your bedtime, alone? Did you both use to lie down together, watch Jimmy Kimmel, and share the events of the day until you both drift off to sleep? But now he opts for a later bedtime, staying up in the den watching reruns of Law and Order until you are soundly in dreamland?

Go see the Doctor: Don't be confused, a sexually transmitted disease would be clear indicator that a husband is having an affair, but in that situation he may be dealing with a whore and not a "GM." The GM's goodies are just as sacred as the wife's. It is natural for women from time to time get a bacterial infection. It can be from soap, sex, or really nothing at all. However, a reoccurring bacterial infection can also mean that someone is dipping his stick in to different pots of gold!

THE LOOK

She's the elephant in the room. She's sophisticated, educated, cute, quiet and quaint. She is a celebrated philanthropist, world renowned, Grammy-winning R&B artist, or maybe even a platinum selling country singer. Perhaps she's an Oscar winning actress. She's a single mother, a daughter, a lover and a fighter. She has no post-secondary education or maybe no education at all. She is government assisted, a hustler by nature, a waitress, a maid, a bartender, a member of the royal family. She doesn't possess the couth or beauty of the coveted Mrs., and she is drop dead gorgeous. She has the heart of a giant. She's a lawyer, a doctor, a politician. She is a receptionist, an administrator, a CEO of a fortune 500. A payday advance getting, check to check living, saint, slut, sinner, eating, praying, loving, Black, White, Red, Yellow, she's a GM.

She's every woman. You know the song... Every woman is subject at her weakest point to entertain thoughts that she otherwise wouldn't have if only she had the strength. Where loneliness and time meet at an impasse and fragility becomes the one. She'd otherwise known better, but knowing sometimes isn't enough. Knowing sometimes isn't even an option. Even with her reputation of making critical decisions and exercising sound judgment in the boardroom, without the least bit of hesitation or reluctance, she is unable to muster up the strength to deny love.

She has no face. She could quite possibly be anybody. Your closest girlfriend, your sister, basketball wife or even at a time in her life, your very own mother, could have been her. It's always entertaining to find out what your mother and or big mama did in a former life before she came to Jesus, of course. It wasn't uncommon for people to have much larger families not so many generations ago. There was always that family, where all the kids looked alike except for those two that were lighter skinned, the ones with the curly hair that took after Grandma's Daddy's side. Families have long endured and kept the family secret that weren't told until long after the death of the matriarch that these children did not belong to Papa at all. They were indeed the man up the street's children, but were treated all the same until they were excluded from the will. Yes, Grandma was a Good Mistress! She never treated her "other" children any differently or gave anyone cause to suspect that they did not belong and dared anyone to say anything otherwise. Not even her husband. It was not to be discussed, ever. As many mistresses do, Granny understood the value of family, as odd as it may seem. She knew that her indiscretions were her own, owned them in silence and carried on.

What's important to realize is it's a misconception that she is the epitome of villain. That is a lie and remains one of the main reasons she is able to fly under the radar. If we don't idolize them, they don't exist. If we don't acknowledge her, she is not valid. That's the general view of wives. If a mistress emerges, it is the goal of the wife to make sure everyone sees the mistress through her eyes. So she will always be a whore, a stripper, ugly and vile. Since shame has erased the true identity, society's only picture is that which has been painted by the wives' hurt and spread by the media. The idea that a mistress "looks" a certain way or fits a certain profile or stereotype such as a party girl, former stripper or local bartender is a ploy used to sell headlines and unfortunately the societal ploy has robbed us of the ability to think rationally and accept that people are not one-dimensional. We are only exposed to Facebook pictures of a man's mistress being a drunken mess at a bachelorette party, or an exposed "sext" message between two consenting adults. It's easy to cast judgment on this woman based on the one sided information. Believe it or not, what you see is not always what you get. The idea that she may be decent is never considered, because let's face it, she made her bed, she's a down trodden, terrible person and oh yeah, decent folks don't sell headlines. Our poor impressionable culture feeds on scandal at the cost of whomever.

  We hear women ask the question all the time, "What does he see in her?" They pose the question superficially as if to suggest that the "she" being the other women were less than attractive in her eyes. At least, this is her hope. This is a systematic way that wives measure their mistresses. She's fat, she's black/ white, she's ugly, and she's this or that, whatever to mitigate her presence. The wife wants to believe that everything about this woman is negative, except that she is real in his life and in fact hers.

Subconsciously, every wife, upon finding out about his mistress questions her own being and potential shortcomings. What does he see in her that he doesn't see in me? An affair, whether it is with a "jump-off" or Good Mistress is a very sobering experience and will wreak havoc on the self-esteem of the seemingly most secure woman. Women will automatically assume she is this drop dead gorgeous cover model or big booty video hoe. Women never consider that her looks has nothing to do with it, perhaps she (the mistress) is just a good person. However it is understandable, how can she be anything of beauty? She (the mistress) is destroying her family.

When she finally puts a face to that gut feeling, a face to a name, a face to the infidelity, she becomes rightfully angry. His mistress will never look like she imagined, because she never imagined her husband cheating on her.

The physical component of the mistress is just the tip of the iceberg. In the event that an affair is exposed, for the wife to suggest that she is less than attractive is normal. This is a stage in the grief process also known as anger. Yes, she very well may be ugly or unattractive. There is a host of unattractive mistress, but this does not disqualify her from being a good one. Although the hurt and opinions of her may be valid, badgering him about how he downgraded will never make him love his mistress any less. It just makes his wife seem shallow and superficial for all intents and purposes. Attacking the beauty and morals of the mistress with the objective to make him feel guilty usually backfires and makes the wife feel even more insecure and insufficient. That is a downside of the ego. That's what hurt people do; hurt people! They deny and assume. It's an attempt by the wife to rationalize the fact that she in on the losing end of an affair. Not necessarily innocent of any wrongdoing but she is the victim. What's puzzling is to think the level of her attractiveness would limit the hurt. If it was with a supermodel, would it have validated his philandering?

Halle Berry is the perfect example of a woman regarded as one of the most beautiful women in the world, not to mention a millionaire. Halle wasn't immune to infidelity. She was married to a R&B singer who allegedly cheated with several women due to a "sex addiction." In instances such as these, it is less about the other woman and more about your man. The point is, one might assume none of the women that he cheated with were more physically attractive than Halle, but nonetheless, they were attractive to him. "One's man trash is another man's treasure." What women may perceive as a beautiful woman outwardly, internally she may be a lousy, miserable bitch and vice versa. Some of the most unattractive women are the most beautiful inside.

"Beauty is in the eye of the beholder." In the moment that he begins to peel back her layers, the moment she tell her truth, her insecurities, her struggles and setbacks, triumphs and victories, that's where he finds beauty. She doesn't have to pretend or play the games, no rings, no strings; she can just be. That is comforting to a man. Especially to a married man, that has lost that connection with his wife. His mistress is refreshing. Men that are in the, "business of marriage" become vulnerable to this woman. It is not her "look," it is her being.

A young man in a conversation was attempting to make a comparison in shopping for oranges and choosing women. He said that he picks his women like he does his oranges. When he shops for oranges, he doesn't pick up the first 2 or 3 that he sees, he finds the most beautiful orange, and that's the one he chooses. He said he has standards. To omit the oranges that may be slightly bruised or misshaped under the guise of standards is careless. Much like woman, the sweetest oranges are the softer, riper ones that are not necessarily always the prettiest ones. While some oranges may be beautiful to the eye, they may be bitter to the taste. The sweeter oranges with the most nutrients are often discarded because most grocers understand that it is the psyche of the average consumer to believe them to be less than perfect. However, every now and then a man comes along, maybe he was in such a hurry, perhaps he was curious or could care less, and he just picks an orange. Upon peeling it he finds the sweetness he has longed for. Men choose their mistress just as they choose their wife. It's important to realize that everyone does not buy oranges for consumption; some just want them for decoration in the fruit bowl. This is the same for a wife or his mistress.

What is "The Look?" The good mistress will always look her very best. She takes special care to make her every impression just as well or better than the first. Where some wives see little value in heels, perfume and lingerie, the GM serves him breakfast in her sexiest six inch pumps. His mistress never misses the opportunity to let him know that his desires are her pleasures to fulfill. And for the wife that is consumed by her image, his desire may be a woman that understands that her best look to him is jeans, t-shirt, and no makeup. Complacency is never an option, in the relationship of the good mistress and him. The secret to her sustainability as a mistress has little to do with her looks, looks are fleeting. She has listened and learned this man. She knows what he likes. That's not to say that physical attraction is not a factor. That would be unrealistic to believe and untrue to write. The majority of the extramarital affairs are born out of some sort of physical attraction. It's human nature for the first attraction between a man and woman to be a physical one. This is the cause of the non-participatory spouse asking the inevitable "What does he see in her?" Unfortunately, he probably never even intended for the affair to take place, he was intrigued by her laugh, her smile, her body, her beauty. Perhaps, she was a co-worker going through a rough patch in life and he needed to feel like the hero he no longer feels like at home. Whatever the case may be, the possibilities are endless but none matter because it is no longer the actual "look" he sees in her. He sees past his mistresses flaws, physically and emotionally. In fact they now share a common flaw that has bonded them both. When he makes the conscious decision to carry on an extramarital affair, it doesn't matter whether she is better or worse than his wife, as smart, pretty or as proper. What he sees when he looks in this woman is far beyond compare. It's beyond any physical standard or rationale. He's sees her in braille. He feels her.

RULES OF ENGAGEMENT

"There's always a right way to do a wrong thing"

~ Unknown

There are rules when one chooses to partake in such a charade. There's almost an unspoken oath or better yet a GM credo that inherently states "You must honor and fiercely protect, but above all else promise to first and foremost, do no harm."

It's never the GM heart's desire to compromise the security of "his" relationship or family. She's very tactful and self-aware. Her lane is never a question as she fully understands her position. There is a particular order and she abides by it wholeheartedly. Some would say that she is able to do this because of her lack of dignity or character, that she has esteem issues or perhaps is a flat out whore. This is the common argument amongst women who find themselves on the other end of the affair. These attacks are baseless in reference to a GM but are more of a defense mechanism, and understandably the sentiment of convenience by those affected.

Contrary to popular belief, to carry on such an illicit affair requires one to be patient, respectful, loyal and understanding. She has to have the innate ability to compromise and an insurmountable measure of self-worth. (Bear in mind we are only referring to the GM). The ability to put the needs of another before your own is foreign in today's society. It is a selfless act, regardless of the circumstance and an attribute to be admired.

It's only fair that we state that while the GM is not completely without fault, there is a so called method to her madness that has absolutely nothing to do with hidden agendas or motives and everything to do with self-preservation. As the bible says, " Behold, I send you forth as sheep in the middle of wolves: be you therefore wise as serpents, and harmless as doves" - Matt 10:16. We like to call the GM's methods, Rules of Engagement.

Rule #1 ~ Call Tyrone

Better yet, call anybody you want to, just not him. A GM is a realist. She understands that there will be no constant contact. Communication may come in the form of a text message, which is always to be diplomatic should she be the initiator and/or at an established time. It is not uncommon for him to contact his person on a daily, weekly or bi-weekly schedule, whatever the frequency they are consistent in nature.

Although communication times vary, what they share is always of substance. The GM is the keeper of his deepest, darkest secrets. The desires that he wouldn't dare share with his wife for fear of judgment or ridicule, so the GM listens with an attentive ear and open heart. Through their communication, he assures her that she is well thought of and will spare no details of the time they have been apart from one another.

If her mode of communication is text, a GM will delete all and we mean all communication between the two and will remind him to do the same. She knows no ends when it comes to keeping what's private, private.

Rule #2 ~ Better to be seen and not heard

There will come a time when you will be with your partner and his wife will call. Period, point blank, it happens. A GM will never under any circumstance tries to discern his tonality to see if they are on the rocks nor will she scrutinize the conversation to use as collateral at a later time. NEVER under any absolute circumstances will she try to be heard or insist that her presence be known. There will be no coughing or giggling or answering of her cell phone, which are to be on vibrate. A GM will do one of two things, she will either sit quietly or try to make the best of an intense situation or she will excuse herself all together. She has the presence of mind and awareness that her time spent is valuable and is to be used wisely. Arguing about trivial issues that are ultimately out of her control is useless. She may not have signed up for the affair, but she signed on for it. This is the nature of the beast. There are no other options. The wife is not in any way her competition and to act as if she is would disqualify her as a Good Mistress.

Consistency is key. The situation has to be handled with such delicacy that should she prove that she has the potential to act any other way than expected, it may result in the demise of the relationship. The idea is not to further complicate an already complicated situation. The GM is not an attention-slore, those roles are best described by the "others". Less is more with this woman if you think about it. The time spent rationalizing the particulars about his relationship with his wife could and would be better spent between the two spending quality time. So with that in mind, she resists the compulsion to sulk, sucks it up and keeps it moving.

Rule #3 ~ Tighten Up

"At the end of the day I don't need a bright woman to argue with, I just want a pretty girl who will shut up when she needs to shut up." Jun Cruz

There will be no whining and crying. In order to maximize the time spent together a GM knows to rid herself of the compulsion to sulk, whine or cry over the small things. It makes for a very uncomfortable encounter and complete waste of time. There will be times when emotions are acceptable and expected. A parent's recent diagnoses with cancer, the death of a childhood friend or family member; these are all acceptable reasons to express emotion. This relationship was built on the most trusting friendship, who else would you bear your soul too. It is not out of the ordinary for him to have to announce that he and his wife are expecting. In situations like that, tears are not completely out the question. Yes, she is a realist and understands that this is a possibility, it comes with the territory, but she is also a human being, not devoid of emotion. However, he, if he knows her, knows what reaction to expect and will proceed accordingly. It is her understanding that the main reasons these relationships even exist is because her person is involved in a loveless relationship bound by obligation. She in no way wants to mimic this behavior. The wife cries, whines and manipulates with her emotions. The GM provides him the oasis of emotional support and a pillar of strength and understanding. No emotional baggage, please.

Rule #4 ~ Cash Rules Everything Around Me

Women who find themselves in this role often find that their man deals in cash. Most will go out of their way to make sure their mistress is kept, but almost always using cash. There will be no traces on his credit card, ever. A paper trail spells disaster.

(Drumroll please…..) And the idiot of the century award goes to John Edwards. Senator John Edwards was on trial for misappropriation of campaign funds to the tune of $925,000. His mistress, Rielle Hunter, with whom he shares a child allegedly, was on the receiving end of some of these funds. This relationship was all kinds of wrong; the money, the child and his sick wife. They were very sloppy. A Good Mistress thinks for the both of them. She is the brains of the operation.

Rule #5 ~ No Love Children

While we are on the subject of John Edwards and his alleged mistress, there were several things that went wrong during the course of this affair. These relationships are emotional affairs and emotions have been known to overpower even people who exercise the soundest of judgment in the entire world. Lawyers, Doctors, Politicians, hell even Astronauts... Remember the diaper lady, Lisa Nowak?

The GM has the responsibility to exercise the best judgment no matter how smitten or jaded. Nothing makes for a messier situation than to bring a child into an already complicated relationship.

For some men his mistress bearing his child, serves as a way out of his loveless marriage. He may encourage her to become pregnant with his love child. . Either the GM is on birth control or for the safety of everyone she ensures they are using protection. A pregnant mistress is a terrible mistress! A GM is smart, she begins with the end in mind and a child almost makes this impossible. A GM's intent isn't to be ruinous and this can and will prove catastrophic to even the strongest bonds. Plus, it's irresponsible. Not for either party, but the child. A GM is not ignorant to the facts of life. She counts the cost and to have a child with this man no matter how much she loves him makes her cringe at the thought. Not only are you putting immeasurable strain on the relationship with him, but that of him and his wife. It denies a child a fair chance at life and a family. The reality is parents hate to hurt their children more than anything in this world. To explain to a child how they came to be honestly, (outside the birds and bees) is hurtful and shameful. A GM knows this and therefore tries to steer clear of it at all cost.

By no means are we stating that if this does happen that it makes a woman a bad person, it just makes you the opposite of a GM. It is hard to abide the code and ethics of being a good mistress when you have a sick kid at home that needs daddy.

Rule #6 ~ Hating Ain't Healthy

A GM never, ever, ever ever criticizes, compares or speaks ill of the wife. To go a step further, the GM never even utters the wife's name. He will complain about her, that's natural, but her job is to listen. There may be moments when the GM will find herself encouraging him to work through their issues, kind of like a pseudo-therapist. A GM will be there to fill her partner's psychological needs and any unsolicited negativity will not only impede progress, but disqualify you as a suitable confidant. A GM is very supportive of her person's relationship, not to sound contradictory or delusional, but this is in fact a part of her role and what separates her from the traditional interpretation of a mistress.

The GM never seeks to make herself feel superior to the Mrs. It's immature, unattractive and unnecessary. To do so gives off an heir of insecurity and the GM is all but insecure. He needs to trust her. The impression that she is insecure is very unsettling for him and would make him reluctant to trust her, her motives and her capacity to handle any potential situation. Also, to attack the wife, is to attack him. A GM knows and understands that this is his wife, his partner and his family. No matter what he is saying about her in confidence and secrecy, there are still two sides to every story. While he may share his side with the GM, the GM must still remain open, never showing judgment based on half of a story. To do so, in his or her favor, would cause her person to recoil. The GM's role is to be his sounding board, knowing at the end of the day, he will always choose his wife.

Rule #7 ~ Two's Company, Three is not an option

If a woman is being "kept" by a man, he will not hear of her seeing another man. A GM is respectful in this aspect, even if she is entertaining the company of another guy, her person will never know. A GM has a sophisticated wit about herself. The elder generation used to say, "Never let your right hand know what your left hand is doing." As contradictory as this may seem, the reality is a woman just can't do what a man can. The idea is that they are in an exclusive relationship, even though he has someone at home. The GM's role is different from that of the legal partner; however "fidelity" is still the expectation.

There are exceptions to every rule. There are GM's who have husbands who find themselves the GM of men with wives. In these situations, both parties understand that the other has another relationship and move forward accordingly with the required care.

The idea, however is that they are in an exclusive relationship committed to the relationship itself. He needs to feel that he has her undivided attention at all times in case it is needed. He needs her to be available at the most inopportune times and to have anyone outside of the obvious may complicate this. Contrary to the stereo-type of most women, men can prove to be very jealous. The mistress having another man makes for very uncomfortable questioning. Is he as good as me? Why didn't you answer when I called you? It leads to him feeling emasculated. In his mind, your loyalty is to him, even if he is married.

Rule #8 ~ Don't pass Go!

If he is a man of means there is a certain image he must portray. The GM will make sure that this image isn't tainted as a result of her existence. For instance if they work in the same office or share a common interest, a GM would do best to forego any public appearance where the 3 would be. It's just risky and uncomfortable for all parties involved. A GM will take it upon herself not to attend.

A GM makes it a further point not to patronize the wife's place of worship, stylist and other places she may frequent such as jewelers, boutiques, etc. out of respect for her. Remember, she is not there to be ruinous, just a victim of circumstance. To have to face this woman in any setting would be very awkward to a woman with any type of dignity. The GM is not void of compassion, the fact the she is unwilling to put herself or the other woman in this situation is proof of it. Where a jump off or groupie would love to see her out and make a public mockery of the marriage, or post banter on the likes of twitter or facebook, display intimate portraits on a paid vacation at his expense, would be altogether enticing for them, but not her. The GM would never enter the home that he and his wife shares. Even if he insist because his wife is out of town, this is a line that she would never cross. The GM does her best to avoid anything that could present such conflict and blatant disrespect. This is not just about her or her partner, but more so out of respect for the Mrs.

Rule #9 ~ *"Keep it lit"*

He experiences a GM in a much different light than all others including the Mrs. It's the forbiddances that makes for such a sweet encounter. No one would want chocolate if it were good for you, neither would they do drugs if it didn't provide for such a high. Fundamentally, that is why mistresses exist. The degree of passion between the two lovers, The GM and her person is undeniable. Plus, there is an impenetrable emotional bond that forms between a man and his GM that creates a beautiful friendship and experience.

He chose her as his GM; she chose to stay on board. This is the understanding moving forward. A GM never seeks this role or these types of men. She is sought. However should she choose to stay in this relationship, it is important to remain the person that he has chosen. When this fact is fully realized is when one moves from ignorance to enlightenment. The GM must always keep the flame lit! She doesn't desire to replace the wife, she chooses to have a confidante, she chooses happiness in the moment or temporary forever, and she chooses a beautiful experience.

Rule #10 ~ Weapons of Mass Destruction

When you think of weapons of mass destruction, you tend to think of missiles, bombs, hand grenades and a number of other weapons used to destroy countries, families and humanity as we know it. However, given the impact social media has had on countries, families, friends and life as we know it, by definition, this term is very fitting.

The social media epidemic has taken us by storm and we were ill prepared and unwilling to learn the rules of engagement before it was too late and it's too late to turn back now. The vast number and popularity of social medium outlets disallows for such acts of infidelity and error to go undiscovered when the wrong players are in the game.

Facebook alone has been cited in over 50% of newly filed divorces. And twitter can account for many of the highly publicized "side-piece" vs wife rants and beefs. Camera phones and 4G coverage, have led to instant exploitation. There should be a course on how to minimize your digital footprint. A man used to only have to arm himself for "he say she say" battles if by some chance his wife was introduced to his affairs. He could always win that fight with "you gonna believe her over me!" Social media is an arsenal that he is unable to contend with.

HER ROLE

Kelly is a stay at home mom, running a mega successful home based business. Her husband is a Controller at a well-known fortune 500 company. Kelly gave birth to twins Jake and Jack 4 years ago and has insecurities concerning her inability to lose the baby weight, she also complains about her husband's long hours at the office and his lack of consideration when it comes to spending time with the children and helping out around the house. She complains that they don't go anywhere together, that he plays video games as if he is a prepubescent teen and is selfish to no end. Apparently, he isn't selfish enough for her to leave him, but this doesn't sound like a relationship anybody with their head on straight would continue in. Or does it?

    A few years back, Kelly was shocked to find out that her husband was having an affair with a woman that was a horrible horrible mistress and person. She taunted Kelly by giving her torturous intimate details about their affair, dates and times of the offenses and recollections of conversations and personal information he had confided in her about his wife, Kelly. Kelly would say that there was absolutely nothing more important than her family and that she had done everything for him and she could not fathom how he could do this to their family and while we are able to empathize with Kelly and her pain, we also can identify with her husband as well.

Men are not robots. They are more like grown boys at best. We don't believe it was ever her husband's intention to hurt her with the affair, most men will honestly say it never is. Men have the uncanny ability to separate the two. His demise lay in the fact that he did not count the cost, should she have found out. This is unfortunate for wives who suffer this fate. While we do not blame women for a cheating husband, we do encourage women to examine their current marital state and identify which areas are lacking and are in need of attention and improvement. She, the wife becomes too relaxed in her position. The ring is only a semblance of where the real work is to begin~

"Marriage is a status, an office" ~ Dietrich Bonheoffer .

Without much further ado, we think that it is only fair that we evaluate the role of the coveted MRS. and what she may have done to perhaps blindly encourage such philandering's. **PLEASE BE ADVISED:** This is in no way placing blame or pointing fingers, it is merely stating that **everyone has a role** and it is time to be open about the role of the wife. If the Loboutin fits, wear them well!

Are you familiar with the cliché, "If it ain't broke, don't fix it?" This applies to cars, home renovations and business plans, not marriage, not ever. We are constantly in flux, growing, learning and changing. We are not the same young girls who were captivated by the antics of the beloved bad boys, we prefer the swag of a gentler man nowadays. As women we change professions, cut our hair, worn it long and even tried it natural. By the same token, once you become married, if you're not conscious, you may become complacent within that relationship forgetting that you yourself are changing and without that presence of mind may find that you and your partner are out of balance and hence growing in different directions.

    Let's face it, marriage can become boring, she becomes bossy, he grows quiet, they become cold and disconnected until the point that you wake up one morning with a "who are you?" look on your face. Sex becomes infrequent, babies must be fed, children must be carted off to school, business meetings must be tended to shortly before we make a quick stop to get the speeding ticket that is being written for going 50 in a 35, all so that we are not late for our 10 year olds football practice. It doesn't stop there, then there's dinner, bath, bedtime … Repeat. Sex? Oh hell no! That is sure to start a fight if he even thinks about asking. The nerve! She's tired, he's horny and that dog hasn't been fed!

    After being on the receiving end of many "It's over, I'm leaving him…I'm done." conversations. We can wholeheartedly say there is a severe disconnect of whom is to blame. Though he may have committed the offense, she most certainly was an enabler and accomplice. Perhaps he was not the only selfish person in the relationship. Had she taken inventory of the relationship and herself, maybe she would have found that she too cheated the marriage and him, just differently. *So, why do women stay in the marriage after the affair?*

The reasons why women stay in marriages after an affair, after they have chosen to forgive or not to forgive may be plentiful. Maybe it's the fear of being alone or being perceived by friends and family as a failure. Perhaps it's the thought that he has learned his lesson and will never do it again. Or simply because she loves him. Whatever the reason, *men who cheat are twice as likely to repeat the offense*. In order for him to repeat the offense would imply that the woman has chosen to stay in the relationship and forgive her mate. Or has she? Staying doesn't equal forgiveness; it's just not the same. A lot of women stay in toxic relationships for the sake of just plain staying or even controlling the men with their guilt. It is the equivalent of emotional entrapment. The first time you are a victim, the second time you are a volunteer.

Few relationships effectively survive the affair. Many stay thinking it's in the best interest of "the kids." Why no one ever addresses how much more damaging it is for children to be in a home with two parents arguing, fussing and fighting is puzzling. Seeing mom cry and walking on eggshells and dad pissed off and subject to kill everybody at any given moment can prove more detrimental to the children than packing up and leaving any day.

Think about your nearest and dearest friend. There isn't absolutely anything in this world that you wouldn't do to make life a little easier for them. You will give them your last dime if need be, pick up their children at a moment's notice, call their mother on her birthday, talk her through the tears of yet another heartbreak, plan a surprise party for their birthday, or take them out for no reason at all, just because. You will listen to them ramble for hours on end about the same man and material she has been talking about for years at a time all in the name of friendship... Now think about your lifetime friend; your mate, how likely are you to perform these same functions? You may do it, but begrudgingly and not without asking if there is sufficient reason that he cannot do it for himself? Are request accompanied with a thousand questions? Do you give attitude or discomfort in him asking you to perform even the most menial tasks on his behalf? Nine times out of ten the honest answer is yes. This alone will make a man feel isolated. There was a point in time where she would travel across the country on a whim should he ask, but at some point after the I do's we seem to lose sight of what is really important, which is the "friendship" aspect of the relationship.

That is the first mistake of the wife. This is the point where she loses sight of **her role as a wife** and allows room for the GM to come in. All relationships with GMs are born out of friendship. And friendship is born out of honor, respect, reverence and trust. At that very moment where the wife makes it uncomfortable for her husband to at the very least communicate with her on ANY level, he will then seek, sometimes even unbeknownst to him, an outlet and that may be in the form of another woman and quite possibly a GM.

It is very vain and irrational for a woman to feel slighted in any way that he sought outside the marriage for someone to talk to, when before she had any inkling of another woman, she would talk about him to anyone who would listen but never engage in any form of substantive dialogue with him. To think that because she bares his last name (but fails to perform her duties as a wife), that she is the only person with intellectual capacity to converse with him is insane.

Here's the truth, treat him like an enemy, he will begin to act like one and at the end of the day, long after the fume of being in love wears off and the marriage license whittles, you are left to deal with the remnants of what was, the reality of what is, and friendship is the absolute only thing that can keep the two together. It's that simple. Men were never created to embody the emotional wherewithal of a woman. Women were created to be nurturers, supportive and caretakers. To become the helpmate of a man **is** not limited to caring for the children and household obligations, but a culmination of all of these things. The same care that is put into caring of a girlfriend should pale in comparison to the support and care that is put into the maintenance of a marriage.

When was the last time you listened, (not to be confused with talking), to him about his dreams? If you had to take time to think about it, the reality is it may be too late. If you haven't given him room to share willingly without provocation, the interaction will seem unnatural to him and he may have grown reluctant to share. Unfortunately for wives, just because he isn't sharing with you, that doesn't mean he isn't sharing. His dreams didn't die; he's just found a new confidante. You have taught him, yes, taught him, through your interaction or lack thereof, how to act towards his GM and react to you. His new confidante has made the easy segue from friend to GM.

A GM allows him to share his feelings and frustrations, dreams and desires without judgment or ridicule freely. A wife on the other hand may see herself bound by obligation and in return reacts negatively to anything foreign that could further upset the family dynamic, therefore keeping it "fresh" and new is not optional. There will be no new businesses that could prove financially risky. He will not introduce any new kinky endeavors inside the bedroom for fear that she may questions where he learned of such perversion. Where the wife will scold him for wanting to do something for himself, because it is not inclusive of the family, the GM understands that we are human, all subject to temporary moments of selfishness. Never under any circumstances should a wife allow herself to become so comfortable that another woman should be able to share in his vision better, sex her man better, suck her man better, feed her man better, make him laugh more, encourage and support his ambition, sext message freakier, love him better, or adore him more. As great as a woman or wife as one may believe herself to be, no one is the best at all things, but the wife's willingness to do all things should be the best! **The role of** the coveted wife is a noble one, however it is an honor and a privilege that left unattended to is not immune to an understudy.

Women of today's society often reject the roles of traditional marriages. We have become a society full of women who know all too well that if we must, we are more than capable of being independent and raising households absent of fathers and can and will if we must. This attitude often spills over into the marriage and she the Mrs.'s thrust herself **into the role of** the man/provider and he is left with a woman who often informs that "she" doesn't need him. Men need to feel needed, it's in his nature. **A GM affirms** his deepest desire by fulfilling this ideal that is inherent in all men. While we have learned that we are his equal, he is still to be reverenced as the head and there are not two heads. Either you are the woman or the man but not both. The inability to submit is the true root of the problem, and until women surrender themselves to the actual role of a wife she leaves herself open.

The death of the ride or die chick often gives birth to the GM. There was a time when his wife was his "ride or die chick." When she would send text messages just to say Good morning and let him know he was being thought of. When she would arrange for steamy sessions on their lunch break or she had butterflies due to the sheer anticipation of an upcoming visit. The times when she could be doing anything anywhere and catch a breath of the scent of his cologne on a nearby co-worker or stranger and instantly begin daydreaming about him, his hugs, his gentle touches, his kiss. What about the endless thoughts of what it would be like to one day be his wife. The names of the children and how many they would have, how he would propose or what was taking him so long? Then, it happen, he proposed, they said their "I do's", and then reality set in. The same man that she would once do absolutely anything under the sun for is now her husband, forever. Now what?

It serves no one in the relationship to hold on to a dream (or love) that no longer nurtures either of you. Hypothetically, what if they are no longer happy? What if, for the sake of this exercise, you knew your dearest friend was unhappy in his/her relationship, what would you suggest they do? You guys are no longer the apple of each other's eye and your every attempt at recovery, be it dressing up or forcing conversation seems very unnatural to the both of you. Yet you force him to remain year after year. Who's the bad guy or girl here? Who are we to deny someone their piece of happiness on earth?

So we blame. We blame the other woman first. We blame her for having no morals, no dignity, no self-respect. We blame her mother for not providing her a father figure. She's this, that and the other. These perceptions are all too outdated as previously stated, everyone **has a role**. Let's be clear, we uphold marriage, but we too embrace reality and the reality is people change. We change our minds as we do our hearts. Picket fences become of less importance and we want the comfort and support of a good person whether it's a wife or good mistress. She, the mistress, too deals with the heartache and heartbreak just like you. As much as wives would like to believe they are better than she is, the term different, is best fitting. The most obvious advice for the mistress would be to just walk away, but what if this "thing" her relationship with him is all she has. What if he is the only man in her entire life that has uttered those three words that every woman longs so desperately to hear? What if, she never had a father figure and her only source of affection and direction was his? Would she be so bad then? Maybe broken, potentially jaded, but never bad. Even if she was a bit selfish, she still made it a point not to disrupt the family or call him at all. She refused to participate in phone games or show up at restaurants where he and his wife would be engaging in an intimate dinner in desperate attempt to distract him and humiliate her by making her feel insecure at the sight of her complete with the same Chanel perfume he bought his wife at her instruction. Would she then be such a bad person? The GM is very careful and thoughtful, as delusional as it may sound. Nine times out of ten her carefulness is not for him, but her, the wife. Because she too is a woman and understands the pain and embarrassment she could suffer and doesn't want that for his wife if she can help it. It's a function of her role as the other party to the relationship. And the best mistresses play their positions well.

"WHAT HE SAID"

The age old saying "there are three sides to every story" applies to the trifold essence of an extramarital affair. In the case of an affair, the three sides are "what he tells his wife, what he tells his mistress, and what he really feels." Reading this book, it may be easy to disregard the words of two women writing about what men feel. There is no education, no experience or no relationship that can give us that insight. However, it's amazing to find what a man, when knowing you don't have any connection to his woman would tell. The game is not always sold; it is quite often told if you listen fast enough.

Below are some examples of random conversations between a male and female co-worker that have a strictly platonic relationship.

Conversation 1

"So the boss is saying that if I stay at this location I will have to switch my hours, which means I will get off later, but if I transfer to the downtown site, I can keep my schedule. I love my hours but I hate that downtown commute!" (male co-worker) "Well what did Michelle say about it?" (female co-worker) "I haven't mentioned it to her; she has so much stress with the kids, and their activities."

Conversation 2

"Happy Birthday Jack!!! I brought you a carrot cupcake your 2nd favorite because I am sure Michelle is probably getting a red velvet cake for you since it's your favorite. What did she get you anyway?" (female co-worker) "Psh, this will probably be my only cake, so thanks ha ha. Oh and my daughter made me a tie out of some shoe strings, that's my princess, I shoulda wore it to work!" (male co-worker) "Well your ass probably don't deserve anything anyway!" (the female co-worker jokes trying to make light of the situation all the while thinking, damn your wife ain't shit, she works and pays no bills, kids are school age but still have a nanny, and she couldn't get a simple gift for a hardworking man that loves his wife and kids!)

Conversation 3

"Well damn, someone looks like they had a long night! How was the date with the new guy?" (male co-worker) "Shit, he was so lame! He don't even watch sports, and you know I wanted to go watch the game! I was home before 9, and had a better time dating myself before I went to bed!" (female co-worker) "Well at least you get to do yourself, I can't watch the game, Michelle ain't giving me none and she won't give me enough time alone to get off on my own" (male co-worker) "What! You lying to me, that's messed up!" (female co-worker)

All three of these conversations are typical coworker banter and not necessarily a telling sign of wrongdoing, but it can be a gateway to an extramarital affair. When a man begins to confide in another woman in areas where he cannot his wife, when another woman begins to do things his wife does not, a window is opened. He loves his wife, but can talk to her (his co-worker) about work, sports and sex. She, his co-worker is having a hard time finding someone to date, and finds herself looking forward to her daily chats with her work friend, who she happens to feel sorry for since his wife is not fucking him. He didn't verbally say he wanted a mistress, but every word **He said** points to an opening.

Most men, single and or married have cheated in their lifetime. In fact, probably every human be it, man or woman has either cheated, is cheating or will cheat. Most people cheat to fill a void. They often believe that the void is one that has been created by their mate, but actually studies show that the void comes from within.

Listed below are some reasons married men told us why they either currently have, they have had or have considered having a mistress:

- My wife nags too much
- We just grew apart
- Ole girl, was fine and she was throwing it at me
- Because I could
- My wife is a whiner
- My wife is needy
- She stopped giving me attention
- I wanted to feel young again
- Everything in life was stress
- I fell in love with someone else
- She's (wife) insecure; she thinks I'm doing it anyway!
- She (mistress) was always my side piece, she was loyal
- She's (mistress) was the one that got away
- It's not natural to be with one person forever
- At first it was just because I wanted a threesome

- I wanted a seed and my wife can't have children
- My wife been together since High School and I wanted to try something different
- My wife betrayed me
- It's cheaper to keep her
- My wife let herself go
- It's all about the kids now, she doesn't pay me any attention
- I don't find her attractive anymore
- I don't like her as a person
- I only married her because we had a baby
- She tricked me into marrying her
- It is acceptable as a part of my culture
- I'm bored with my marriage
- She doesn't satisfy me sexually

All a man has are "his balls and his word" the balls are the same regardless of which way they swing but the words mean different things to the women he shares them with! Man gives his wife his word; he gives his mistress *his word*!

He says he will love and give of himself to only her.
He says I got you.
He says he will honor her.
He says he will protect you.
He says he loves his red bone.

He says the darker the berry the sweeter the juice.
He said that he never would date outside of his race.
He said I can't deal with these Black women.
He says that he will never hurt you.
He said he is the only one that will love you this much.
He said he appreciates you.
He said you are his light.
He said he doesn't smile until he sees your face.
He said I would never give anyone your loving.
He said I barely touched her.
He says baby come handle some of your wifely duties.
He says I haven't slept with her in months.
He says you and the kids are my world.
He said I am only there for the kids.
He said you are my soul-mate.
He said I prayed for you.
He said I prayed for us.
He said these things to someone; choose one!
He says I LOVE you! He says I LOVE you! He says I LOVE you!

FROM GUILTY TO FORGIVEN

"Guilty as charged! I did it! There you have it!" Her soul wells up and burst forth in a steady flow of tears. She shrinks, shrugs her shoulders, closes her eyes and with a slow deep breath, exhales, you're right! This announcement followed by an overwhelming flood of emotion as she pleads, I am guilty. I am guilty of loving a married man and unfortunately, yes, that man, is your husband. I am guilty of thinking of him every single morning when I open my eyes only to realize he is not here beside me, to hold me, to wish me a good day and send me off into this unkind world with the gentle kiss on the forehead that he does. Just as I am guilty for allowing him to penetrate my every thought before I close my eyes each night and more than my thoughts, also my body. The thoughts and images of him which are reserved for you only, I am guilty of too thinking. His victories I celebrate the same way you do, his defeats leave me defeated. The big games, the bad media, the promotions and reprimands, the milestones, peaks and valleys, yes he calls me too. I've kept his secrets just as I've also kept him sane.

I was there to talk him through the knock down drag out fights the two of you've had about any and everything. It was me that coaxed him into to calming down and returning home to apologize to you. I'm selfish and a hypocrite; I own this. I'm guilty of being jealous of other women that may have caught his attention as if it were my place to be upset. I know, it's complicated, but you have to understand I never meant for it to be this way.

What you must think of me, and my God, your children... They are sure to never forget the look on your face when realized your worst fears had come true. That very moment you confirmed that it was another woman, me, that was the cause of him staying out late, neglecting you, and making you feel isolated and alone. It was me that contributed to you feeling like less a woman and definitely not his soul mate or wife.

I flew to meet him in San Francisco, Chicago, London, Nigeria and Melbourne. That's why he insisted it wasn't that big of deal and that you didn't need to trouble yourself to attend. Yes, at times the lipstick on his collar may have been an accident from a platonic embrace of a female coworker, but not often. Yes it was mine, and yes he has been carless at times. Yes, yes, yes, it's all true. Does that make you feel better? Was this what you were looking for? Is this what you so desperately needed to hear? Well, now you know the truth. Yes, I've done what you say I did, and probably more than you could ever imagine, but I'm just not who you say I am. This is what the truth would sound like, if only the GM had the courage to tell.

Judgment

In the New Testament, the book of John introduces us to an adulterous woman. This particular woman was brought before Jesus, but not first without being persecuted, man handled and drug through the streets like a wild animal. Imaginably, she was filthy and bloodied from the abuse suffered at the hands of people she knew and loved dearly. People, whom surely she at one point in time or another broken bread with, celebrated life's memories and milestones, cared for and prayed with, only to be mercilessly humiliated by without a second thought. The scripture reads:

"Teacher, this woman was caught in the act of adultery. The Law Moses commanded us to stone such women. Now what do you say?" (John 8:4-5)

We are willing to bet that she wished she had been stoned to death already or anything to get it over and done with. You've disrespected me, belittled me, spat on me, cursed my name, called me every whore you can think of, killing me would be doing me a favor, she probably hoped.

One point of interest in this verse and worthy of pointing out is that they were already clear on what the laws were. They were indisputable. They didn't have to take her anywhere. She was an adulterer, and fit to be stone to death on the spot. The offense of adultery was punishable by death and yet even with all this information, "they" obviously were uncomfortable and honestly unfit to carry out the punishment without first consulting "THE TEACHER."

The verse goes on to read that Jesus would then go on to bend down and write on the ground with his finger as they continued to question him. Finally, "He straightened up and said to them, 'If any one of you is without sin, let him be the first to cast the first stone.'" (John 8:7-8). Oh, and then he continued to write on the ground.

Wow, what a statement. He seemed so cool and unconcerned, with so much confidence that he already knew what was to come next; nothing! No one would be able to cast that stone.

It goes on to tell how the crowd would eventually thin to nothing. The older, wiser men cleared first. The younger ones would then follow suit and trickle away. After much self-examination, not one was qualified to make such a judgment call. Not one! Not the older, the wiser, the more experienced of the people nor the young. The crowd was cleared to absolutely no one. No one but her and her Jesus remained.

It's almost as if today's culture has taken a page right out of this particular scripture of events. However, unlike the scripture, instead of dragging this woman through the streets she now is drug through cyberspace and never brought before Jesus. Her judgment or half assed attempts at a lesson is done by trying to shame her into changing her bad behavior. Luckily for the woman in the bible, the adulterous woman, they brought her to the right place.

"Jesus straightened up and asked her, 'Woman, where are they? Has no one condemned you?'"

"No one, sir,"

They had all gone on their way

"Then neither do I condemn you," Jesus declared. "Go now and leave your life of sin" (John 8:10-12).

It wasn't until the woman was brought before Jesus that she would be able to face her sin head on and to everyone's surprise, he had compassion for her, just like he said he would. The heartache and pain and all that she had endured to get to this point. The hills she had to climb literally, the embarrassment and shame she had suffered and just like that, he forgave her. Right there on the spot, the sin was no more. Was she guilty of being with a married man, yes! Was God aware? Yes. Was she forgiven??? Absolutely!

Guilt is an absolute fact. There is no gray area. The GM is guilty for her role in an extra marital affair. You're either guilty or not guilty in relation to the legal or moral code you govern yourself by. **Shame** for the virtuous, is guilt's by- product. It's the emotional counterpart of guilt, however unlike guilt (which is the conviction all parties involved in affairs own), shame is the sickening feeling in the pit of your stomach that relentlessly insists that, yes you are a bad person! That feeling is reserved only for the "Good Mistress." Not all people engaged in affairs feel this, not all people have a conscience. Shame takes guilt to another level that says, I am a wretched, worthless home wrecker, suitable for no one except for half a man. Shame tells you that you are not good enough to be a wife.

Shame left unexpressed and unaddressed is devastating for everyone. It's that bad angel on your shoulder that constantly whispers in your ear, how terrible of a human being you are. Shame is a sickness whose only purpose is to keep you in bondage and broken. And while the GM should not be immune to punishment just because she is "good" and realizes that she has done wrong, the question is what is a suitable punishment and who is qualified enough to decide what punishment would be greater than the voice on her shoulder. Should a life of shame be an absolute sentence or are we as a society ready to deal with this issue like adults in an earnest attempt to heal and move forward? The bottom line is we are all human, we all make mistakes, we all have feelings that change and all these things are the nucleus of an affair.

Shame is born out of fear, the fear of being unaccepted, and the fear of being rejected, unloved or judged. Shame exists because we become afraid of facing the demons, because they've always said "it's your fault, you created this hell!" You made the decision, you made your bed, now lay in it. Because shame depends on secrecy for its survival she remains broken because what has caused the shame, her affair, also thrives on secrecy. She is unable to untangle the knots of her soul, unable to unpack the anxiety and worry that this has created in her, because after all, who can she tell? Aside from him, because this is their common flaw, who would ever understand the stain infidelity has left on her soul? No one cares about the hole this has left in her heart, or so she tells herself. The finger shaking and disproval by loved ones who are sworn to love her, the cut of the eye like knives by supposed friends and the proper wives, are of course imagined, because she has yet to even tell her side of the story. All of these things are too much to fathom so she resigns herself to hopelessness and ill imagined thoughts, ie. shame.

Regret

The account of the biblical adulterous woman teaches us an ultimate lesson in forgiveness. It also teaches us a valuable lesson about casting judgment on one another, but what does this lesson teach us about judging *ourselves*? An affair is wrong. That is understood and it is indisputable. GM's have never maintained that they are innocent of their part in an affair. GM's understand that they too have a role in the infidelity, though not the cause and it is important that we drive this point in defense of the GM, as they are not the perpetrator. Nonetheless, they, the GM, too have a role and because of this she has been the subject of many blogs, hot topic conversations, headlines and heartbreaks. What is unfairly depicted is the representation of these women is the portrayal that she is a spineless, reckless, wretched individual without moral or duty.

GM's have a heart and she too gets hurt in an affair. While this may seem like a very hard pill to swallow, not only does the wife suffer the ill of a marriage gone awry, but believe it or not, the mistress gets hurt just as much and at times even more. Not only because of the possibility of her loved ones reconciliation of the marriage, should they discover the affair proved useful to their union, but for what the affair has done to her core, her character in general and she regrets it.

Her regret is what makes her human. Believe it or not, GM's see the error in their ways and choices. She has her regrets. She often wishes she could go back in time and right the wrong and she so desperately wants to be forgiven. A GM regrets the missed opportunities to express her hearts deepest desires, to love her person completely, without regard or regret. She regrets that moment when she realized that this was not a possibility and the fact that she didn't run for the hills. She regrets the way they met and by the same token she wouldn't take it back, even if she could. There are also the days that she regret ever telling him to marry her, yes some GM's existed as friends far before the wives! There's always that little voice that recalls the conversation, oh no, that's him that always reminds her that she was the one that told him to do it, to marry her, in the first place. In a moment of passion and drunken honesty, she did. Was it because she believed his good wholesome girl was a better fit? That maybe she had a little too much baggage for him. She regrets that she put his ego and her insecurity before herself. She regrets that she loved him so much and so damn hard, that is made her deaf, blind and mute to what was really happening. She regrets that she enjoyed being with him so much, because she knew there was someone at home who loved him just as much and honestly, probably even more than she. There was someone who missed him, someone who worried about him too. She regrets that she believed in his love, and the fact that he chose her in essence would never be enough for her to leave him.

    She regrets that she had to bring her sister as her plus one to weddings and the company holiday party. She regrets the many times she had to drop her son off to stay at G-Ma house for a last minute impromptu get away with him. She regrets that her daughter ask who he was often as they talked on the phone and she said no one, because he was most definitely someone and contributed to her everyday life. She regrets that her son knew him as an "uncle" pretty much all of his life. She regrets that she was her parent's only child, and to them she could do no wrong and as devout Christians they anxiously awaited the day to marry their daughter off. She often wondered if they would think she was a terrible person or mother. So much regret, she knew it was wrong, but she loved this man with her every fiber and he loved her. He loved the unlovable parts, the broken pieces, the insecure moments and all of her regrets. He made them all better, but simply... He was a married man."

She regretted every time she woke up from the nightmare of running into his wife face to face and she ask her if she is fucking her husband! She couldn't ever reasonably expect her to forgive her, at best she would hope that she would have some type of epiphany moment and at least understand how she too fell for the same charming, genuinely caring and incredibly handsome young man. She regrets in the moments of this reoccurring nightmare, when she was prepared to walk away forever, he wouldn't let her. It was always her birthday, or Christmas, Mother's day or some holiday that would give him a reason to call as if he needed a reason at all. Anytime he felt her drifting too far away, he would come back for her. She regrets picking up the phone. She regrets what it would do to her, but would his wife care enough to understand any of this? And honestly, could anyone blame her?

The GM's regrets are because she is a creature of twisted consciousness; a GM will not only bear the burden of having to face the public shame and humiliation of being a man's mistress but the negative self-abuse as a result of the affair as well. Unable to forgive herself for what she has done, she is constantly haunted by her skeletons. The guilt, the overwhelming feelings of powerlessness and fear that render her helpless, are an inherit trait of any GM. The notion that karma is always around the next corner is forever present. The idea that the proverbial bomb is about to drop at any given time is a constant worry. And if the self-affliction of ridicule is not enough, it's accompanied by criticism of others through the media monsters, the inaccurate accounts by the "good wives", southern belles, tweeters, facebookers and bloggers united. The lingering of the noise and the sting of the condemnation stems from memories of the bad decisions that she has made, things she's done, places she's been, and brokenness she's had to endure because of her very own choices and because of this she is unable to forgive herself. So be that as it may, while she would like to ask the wife for her forgiveness, she would first need to accept the forgiveness of God and then herself, before anything constructive can ever take place.

Forgiveness

"Jesus straightened up and asked her, "Woman, where are they? Has no one condemned you?" "No one, sir," she said. "Then neither do I condemn you," Jesus declared. "Go now and leave your life of sin" (John 8:10-12).

God's forgiveness is free. It is only required that we ask and then receive but only after we fulfill our part which is to forgive and ye shall be forgiven. Often times, we ask God for things, but we lack the capacity to believe that he has honored our requests.

"Forgiving this woman, this monster, will make her think what she has done to me and my family ok."

It is understandable at first thought for a wife to think it is absurd to forgive her husband's mistress. Contrarily, keeping this woman in a constant state of shame will do nothing to undo the action or rid the hurt she caused. The wife believes shaming her, embarrassing her in public, belittling her to anyone within an ears distance keeps her in her place like a caged beast. Forgiving does not mean that you are ok with what happened, however it would allow the burden to be lifted from your own heavy heart. Forgiveness is freeing. It is impossible to move towards a happy healthy relationship with a spouse while still holding the emotional pain and baggage caused by an affair. The only way to grow is to put it out on the table; ignoring the fact that another woman was once a part of your husband's life is not a realistic solution. Neither is badgering him about the details nor reminding him every opportunity you get of his betrayal. Nagging grows tiresome; remember he has established an emotional relationship with the GM, so guess who he's going to call when the wife is getting on his nerves. You guessed it. Forgiving her will not make her assume that the affair was ever ok and it will not excuse her actions.

Forgiving your mistress (yes yours, because in marriage what is his is yours) will cause her to actually own what has happened. It is a devastating blow to learn of an affair, but women stay down long after the initial blow because they refuse to own that this is happening to them. Not their family, but themselves. It's a bitter pill to swallow. The realization that as his wife, and as good of a woman she may have been to him, she was not his only one. It's easier to reject the truth, but disowning it doesn't make this other woman disappear. Confronting your feelings about the affair and working through the feelings with the goal to forgive will eventually make the feelings of hatred for her and the emptiness within go away.

Forgiveness doesn't mean letting go of what has happened, it means letting go of your obsession and the illness it has caused you. Forgiveness is a sign of growth and because this is one of the most damaging things that can happen in life, the ability to forgive the other party is a sign of grace and integrity.

"If I forgive her, they may do it again."

Withholding forgiveness as a form of punishment only imprisons oneself. When you don't forgive you allow misery to live within yourself. In an attempt to sentence someone for the wrong you suffered as a result of their action, by not forgiving you are confined to that same prison. It will cause you to become bitter and unloving towards not only your spouse but others around you. To forgive literally means to untie. The pinned up frustration and hatred must be unbound in order to live a life of freedom. It is not required to make amends with the mistress, but amends with your thoughts, actions and feelings about her. And it is important to note that withholding forgiveness is not a guarantee that "it" will never happen again.

"She is nothing like me; I would NEVER do this to anyone."

Forgiveness takes courage. Just as it takes courage to be bold and say, yes I am guilty of what you say, by the same token it takes that same amount of courage to respond to the hatred by saying to the mistress," I forgive you." The forgiveness from the wife is not only for the mistress, but for herself, the wife, and the feelings she has allowed the affair to create in her. Hatred, envy, and evil has taken residency in her heart because of a mistake; the affair. She has to forgive herself for the little part of herself that she deep down feels may have contributed to the affair. Have you ever made a mistake? I will answer this for you, yes! This means the wife and the mistress and the rest of us all have something in common. Regardless of what the mistake was, no one is perfect. Have you ever hurt another person without intention? Have you ever needed forgiveness?

When Jesus instructed the townsmen to by all means, stone her, with one condition, and in the end it was just her and her Jesus, it says that his forgiveness was the only forgiveness this woman ultimately needed. The wife forgiving the GM may feel good to know for the mistress, but ultimately the wife forgiving the GM is for her own sake.

THE GOOD MISTRESS' APOLOGY

Dear Mrs.,

 With my heart in hand, I offer every wife my sincerest regret for any ill suffered by my acts or any other good mistress and your husbands. We carelessly invaded the stability and sanctity of your marriage. Though you may have suffered the embarrassment and hurt, I forever carry the burden of what this act did to our lives. I never wished this upon you. I didn't seek you out to purposely destroy you. Though my desire to protect everyone involved did not supersede my ability to say no and walk away, please believe that the intent was always there to do so. Sometimes good intentions are just never ever quite enough. But for just one moment, may I challenge you to look deeper. There are so many nuggets of wisdom that can be learned even from the exposure of this harsh truth. You probably don't want to hear anything I have to say but…What you and he have is sacred, it is a covenant ordained by god. Your love is worth the fight, or else I would not exist as a mistress; I would be his girlfriend. He would have left you and your family. I apologize if I have caused you to question your worth. I apologize if I created that pain in your gut. I apologize for your sleepless nights. This was never about you, you did nothing to deserve this. Some things just are as they are.

Sincerely,

A Good Mistress

DEAR GOOD MISTRESS

Dear Good Mistress,

Let me begin by saying you are not bad! Your behavior, yes, but you absolutely are not. This is such a small piece of who you are and it is a part of your story you must own in order to move forward in true love and grace. It's time to forgive yourself, after all God forgives you. You no longer have to be defined by the values they place on you, but by the values you place upon yourself. You have to have a grander vision for yourself, even queens sometimes behave badly. I am not giving you an excuse, just oxygen. You are still a queen no matter what they say, and no matter the lies you've told yourself. "They" have their secrets they are also ashamed to tell. You are not alone. You are not the only one who has been guilty of loving someone with your entire heart only to be misunderstood. We know what it feels like to want nothing more than to be loved and accepted only to have the only person that loves and accepts you exactly how you are, not be completely available. We know you loved for loves sake and not in spite of another. We know that your hearts true intention was to honor that which was sacred to her, but for whatever the reason, it just didn't work out that way. There is so much good and richness that dwells in you my love and don't believe anything otherwise about yourself. You are still created in his image. Your still Gods most prized possession and there is such a thing as a "good" mistress; you are her. Fix your crown... You have to stop beating yourself up over this. Accept God's forgiveness and do it now! Stop making excuses about why you can't find a man, that you've done too much bad in the world and lives of others. That he will cheat on you because you've ruined a family, or have cheated with someone. The slate has been wiped clean. Go now and leave your life of sin as he instructed you to do. The cat is out of the bag, so be a fierce lioness! Inhale, exhale and let the light in. You no longer have to be burdened by the shame. Who cares how you got here, damn the circumstances. Declare that you will be kinder to yourself, gentler with yourself. What's done is done, make amends and move on. Your own spirit of insufficiency limits you.... Use that same spirit to overcome... You may have thought there was something wrong with you, that you were bad and irreparably damaged, LIES!!!! Don't punish yourself for a sin God had already forgiven.

    People can be cruel and unjust. The measuring sticks we use to judge each other are so skewed, as if one sin is worse than others because the poison is different. All sin is sin. Didn't you keep his secrets? Well that made you an incredible confidante! Look at the silver lining, if you change the way you look at things the things you look at will change! If you believe no one will love you if your secret is exposed, begin with loving yourself!

MEDITATIONS FOR THE GOOD MISTRESS

"Come now, and let us reason together, saith the LORD: though your sins be as scarlet, they shall be as white as snow; though they be red like crimson, they shall be as wool." ~ **Isaiah 1:18**

"If we confess our sins, he is faithful and just to forgive us our sins, and to cleanse us from ALL unrighteousness." ~ **1 John 1:9**

"As far as the east is from the west, so far hath he removed our transgressions from us." ~ **Psalms 103:12**

"Who gave Himself for us to redeem us from EVERY lawless deed, and to purify for Himself a people for His own possession, zealous for good deeds." (NASB) ~ **Titus 2:14**

"In whom we have redemption through his blood, the forgiveness of sins, according to the riches of his grace;" (The word 'riches' in the Greek here means abundance and fullness!) ~ **Ephesians 1:7**

"There is therefore now no condemnation to them which are in Christ Jesus..." ~ **Romans 8:1**

"...he will have compassion upon us; he will subdue our iniquities; and thou wilt cast all their sins into the depths of the sea." ~ **Micah 7:19**

"Bless the LORD, O my soul, and forget not all his benefits: Who forgiveth all thine iniquities; who healeth all thy diseases; Who redeemeth thy life from destruction; who crowneth thee with lovingkindness and tender mercies;" ~ **Psalms 103:2-4**

The Lord is near to those who have a broken heart and saves such as have a contrite spirit. ~ **Psalm 34:18**

EXTRAS

Famous or Infamous Mistress in History

(Not all were "Good Mistress")

Cleopatra: She had an affair with Mark Anthony while he had a wife

Marilyn Monroe: She had an affair with John F. Kennedy and the world remembers her infamous Happy Birthday serenade

Elizabeth Taylor: The list is end list but she was rumored to have had affairs with JFK as well as Ronald Reagan

Amy Fisher: Was the 17 year old known as the "Long Island Lolita," her infamous affair with the married Joey Buttfuoco proved deadly for his wife

Lucy Mercer: She lived from 1891 to 1948 and is best known for her affair with President Franklin D. Roosevelt

Rachel Uchatel: Of all of the women that attempted at their 5 minutes of fame from their romps with Tiger Wood, Rachel was the closest thing to an actual mistress.

Daisy Wright: Is one of the first nanny affairs that was brought to light publically when news broke that she was having an affair with her employer Jude Law while he was married

Mildred Baena: The mistress of actor, turned governor Arnold Schwarzenegger. She also mothered a secret love child with him.

Rielle Hunter: Had the affair with John Edwards while his wife battled cancer. The love affair got more unwanted attention when it was found that he misappropriated campaign funds to take care of her.

Oksana Grigorieva: The mistress of Mel Gibson. Mel fathered her child while still being married. Their relationship caught public attention with the highly publicized break-up and acrimony.

Mistress that got the ring!

Alicia Keys: Was allegedly the mistress of DJ and producer Swizz Beats while he was still married to Mashanda. These allegations seem to have holes, but at the end of the day, Beats and Keys are now married with a son.

Camilla, Duchess of Cornwall: The current wife of Prince Charles of Wales allegedly began their love affair while he was still married to Princess Diane.

LeAnn Rimes: This mega country star married actor Eddie Cibrian after they were both exposed for an affair that sparked while they were both married and filming a movie together

Angelina Jolie: The now Mrs. Jolie-Pitt is said to have led to the demise of Hollywood's the Golden Couple, Jennifer Aniston and the Brad Pitt.

Julia Roberts: This "Pretty Woman" and now wife of Danny Moder supposedly met him on the set of the movie 'The Mexican". Danny was allegedly married at the time, however he has since divorced and put a ring on it.

Gabrielle Union: Because Dwayne Wade was still technically married when he and Gabrielle allegedly began dating; it's only fair that she makes the list. His ex-wife felt so strongly about this that she actually brought suit against the actress which was eventually thrown out court.

COMING SOON......

When The Good Mistress
Goes Bad

For the latest updates and new releases...

Follow The Good Mistress:
Twitter: good_mistress
Instagram: good_mistress

www.ingramcontent.com/pod-product-compliance
Lightning Source LLC
Chambersburg PA
CBHW032054150426
43194CB00006B/520